REBUILD

A STUDY IN
NEHEMIAH

KATHLEEN NIELSON
with D.A. CARSON

LifeWay Press®
Nashville, Tennessee

Published by LifeWay Press ® • © 2014 The Gospel Coalition

ISBN: 978-1-4300-3223-6

Item: 005644872

Dewey Decimal Classification: 222.8

Subject Headings: BIBLE. O.T. NEHEMIAH--STUDY \ GOD--WILL \PROVIDENCE AND GOVERNMENT OF GOD

Scripture quotations are from The Holy Bible, English Standard Version® (ESV®), copyright © 2001 by Crossway, a publishing ministry of Good News Publishers. Used by permission. All rights reserved.

To order additional copies of this resource, order online at www.lifeway.com; write LifeWay Small Groups: One LifeWay Plaza, Nashville, TN 37234-0152; fax order to 615.251.5933; or call toll-free 1.800.458.2772.

Printed in the United States of America

Adult Ministry Publishing

LifeWay Church Resources

One LifeWay Plaza

Nashville, TN 37234-0152

PRODUCTION TEAM

WRITER:
KATHLEEN NIELSON

EDITORIAL PROJECT LEADER:
BRIAN DANIEL

ART DIRECTOR:
JON RODDA

EXECUTIVE EDITOR:
COLLIN HANSEN

GENERAL EDITOR:
D.A. CARSON

CONTENT EDITORS:
GENA ROGERS, SPENCE SHELTON

PRODUCTION EDITOR:
MEGAN HAMBY

EXECUTIVE PRODUCER:
BEN PEAYS

VIDEO PRODUCER & EDITOR:
TIM COX

VIDEO DIRECTOR:
TIM COX

DIRECTOR, ADULT MINISTRY:
FAITH WHATLEY

DIRECTOR, ADULT MINISTRY PUBLISHING:
PHILIP NATION

CONTENTS

ABOUT THE GOSPEL COALITION

The Gospel Coalition is a fellowship of evangelical churches deeply committed to renewing our faith in the gospel of Christ and to reforming our ministry practices to conform fully to the Scriptures. We have become deeply concerned about some movements within traditional evangelicalism that seem to be diminishing the church's life and leading us away from our historic beliefs and practices. On the one hand, we are troubled by the idolatry of personal consumerism and the politicization of faith; on the other hand, we are distressed by the unchallenged acceptance of theological and moral relativism. These movements have led to the easy abandonment of both biblical truth and the transformed living mandated by our historic faith. We not only hear of these influences, we see their effects. We have committed ourselves to invigorating churches with new hope and compelling joy based on the promises received by grace alone through faith alone in Christ alone.

We believe that in many evangelical churches a deep and broad consensus exists regarding the truths of the gospel. Yet we often see the celebration of our union with Christ replaced by the age-old attractions of power and affluence, or by monastic retreats into ritual, liturgy, and sacrament. What replaces the gospel will never promote a mission-hearted faith anchored in enduring truth working itself out in unashamed discipleship eager to stand the tests of kingdom-calling and sacrifice. We desire to advance along the King's highway, always aiming to provide gospel advocacy, encouragement, and education so that current- and next-generation church leaders are better equipped to fuel their ministries with principles and practices that glorify the Savior and do good to those for whom He shed His life's blood.

We want to generate a unified effort among all peoples—an effort that is zealous to honor Christ and multiply His disciples, joining in a true coalition for Jesus. Such a biblically grounded and united mission is the only enduring future for the church. This reality compels us to stand with others who are stirred by the conviction that the mercy of God in Jesus Christ is our only hope of eternal salvation. We desire to champion this gospel with clarity, compassion, courage, and joy—gladly linking hearts with fellow believers across denominational, ethnic, and class lines.

Our desire is to serve the church we love by inviting all our brothers and sisters to join us in an effort to renew the contemporary church in the ancient gospel of Christ so we truly speak and live for Him in a way that clearly communicates to our age. As pastors, we intend to do this in our churches through the ordinary means of His grace: prayer, ministry of the Word, baptism and the Lord's Supper, and the fellowship of the saints. We yearn to work with all who seek the lordship of Christ over the whole of life with unabashed hope in the power of the Holy Spirit to transform individuals, communities, and cultures.

In its Women's Initiatives, The Gospel Coalition aims for gospel renewal specifically among and through the women of the church. We desire to support the growth of women in faithfully studying and sharing the Scriptures; in actively loving and serving the church; and in spreading the gospel of Jesus Christ in all their callings. Women benefit from and contribute to The Gospel Coalition's resources in many ways—on the website, in conference settings, and in various publishing projects. We pray that, through the Women's Initiatives, Jesus will be glorified and the church will be strengthened.

FOREWORD

One of the decisions that the Board of The Gospel Coalition made a couple of years ago was to better integrate some of the things we try to do. One of the consequences of this decision was to tie the plenary addresses of our major conferences to Bible study materials that could easily be used by local churches. That is why the 2013 National Conference, which in its plenaries focused on the Gospel of Luke, prepared a short Bible study book on this Gospel, complete with video messages, study questions, and the like. Our hope is that the material will be used in Sunday Schools and small groups. Obviously it can be linked with the video messages and with the videos of the plenary sessions from the 2013 conference—videos that can be downloaded at no expense from our website (*thegospelcoalition.org*).

The book you hold in your hand is our attempt to do something similar for the plenaries of the Women's Conference (June 2014). The biblical focus of the plenaries is the Book of Nehemiah. With her experience of providing material for women's Bible studies, Kathleen Nielson was the ideal person to write this study, designed to be used in small groups and Sunday School classes. She provides enough material to plunge readers into the text, to listen to what the Bible actually says, without swamping readers with more material than they can usefully absorb. Once again TGC has provided video messages, and once again these studies will benefit from watching these messages as well as the videos of the plenary sessions.

Above all, we are eager for Christians to know God and His Word better, not least in the framework of the entire Bible, so that they can see for themselves how God in Scripture sovereignly traces out the story of His redeeming purposes in such a way that all the lines of thought, all the trajectories, all the elements of the complex plots, come together in Jesus Christ.

Don Carson

INTRODUCTION

In Nehemiah, the curtain is going down on Old Testament history, and we get one last glimpse—one last compelling story. It's the story of a remnant of God's people who returned to Jerusalem after their exile, led by Nehemiah to rebuild the city wall. As Nehemiah tells the story, we see not only the wall rebuilt, but the people of God rebuilt around God's Word. This is the people God promised to bless, and through whom God promised blessing for all the peoples of the earth. Nehemiah shows us that God's promises do not fail. God is faithful, according to His Word.

Nehemiah sounds the call for God's people to live by God's Word. At a weak and struggling point, in a broken-down and deserted city, they are called to walk by the light of the Word. As we read about both their joyful obedience and their frustrating failures, we understand that we are reading our history as God's people now. As we perceive how the story of Nehemiah's time finds its place in the unfolding biblical plotline, we see most of all God's steadfast love in planning redemption for a people who disobey His Word. Reading Nehemiah, we savor more deeply the fulfillment of all God's promises in the coming of His Son to deliver a people fully and finally from the bondage of sin.

The Book of Nehemiah takes us to a crucial point in salvation history, from which we must look both back and ahead. In light of all the Old Testament stories that come before, we see how poor and little is this remnant of the people who grew from Abraham's seed into a great kingdom just as God promised—and who then seemed to lose all their greatness. Now these few are simply subjects of a foreign king. God's promises, however, point not to the greatness of this people among the nations but to the greatness of the One who would come from them to bless all the nations. That One would be an eternal King in the line of David. Here at the Old Testament's close, there is no earthly kingdom in sight. God's people are left with His Word. They must return to it. They must live and worship in obedience to its teachings. As Nehemiah reestablishes this remnant within Jerusalem, restoring their temple worship with its priests and sacrifices, we cannot help but look ahead—to Christ our great High Priest who by means of His own blood secured for us an eternal redemption (see Heb. 9:11-12). The temple and priests point us forward to the One in whom we can draw near to God, through His sacrifice on our behalf. As the curtain closes on Old Testament history, Nehemiah points us right to Jesus.

This study opens up the riches of Nehemiah through eight sessions: one introductory session of overview and context, followed by seven sessions that take us right through the book. The study grew out of our planning for The Gospel Coalition 2014 National Women's Conference, and sessions 2-8 follow the breakdown of chapters and titles used in the conference plenary talks, based on Nehemiah. Our prayer has been that the conference would help awaken an interest to dig in further and to dig in with others—hence this study. Three of the plenary speakers from the conference (Don Carson, Nancy Guthrie, and Kathleen Nielson) have prepared the videos that accompany each of the sessions in this study. We hope these video messages will help you do some further fruitful digging into this rich Old Testament narrative. The Book of Nehemiah itself calls us as God's people to come together with minds and hearts focused on learning and following God's Word.

How should this study be used? Following the format of *The Gospel of Luke: From the Outside In* (published in coordination with The Gospel Coalition 2013 National Conference), these sessions are group-friendly—accessible, we hope, both for a person new to the Scriptures and for one with a fair deal of experience. There is huge benefit in the fellowship of such people digging in together. Each session offers a combination of commentary that sets the stage and questions that draw us deeper into the text—to observe what it says, to find its meaning in context, and to ask how we should apply that meaning today. The sessions will be most beneficial if participants do some preparation in advance. However, for the ones who may just come (and for all of us), we can pray that God's inspired Word will do its work of penetrating hearts like the sharp, two-edged sword that it is. The primary focus, then, must be on the process of listening carefully and prayerfully to the Word and going away with it echoing in our hearts and minds.

These sessions will prepare you to dig deeper; they will help with the groundwork. We hope that you will go on to do more in-depth study of the text yourself, searching out its words and themes and shape from beginning to end. Studying the Word is a life-long process, one in which we must continually aim to bring others along with us. May this study contribute to that process in the lives of God's people, by God's grace.

ABOUT THIS STUDY

PREPARATION

Group members are encouraged to prepare as much as possible each week in advance—first and foremost by a careful reading of the biblical text covered in that week's session. The **Introduction** to each session leads into the **Scripture** text. You'll want to have a Bible on hand to read the text for the week right at the start and to refer to as you make your way through the lesson. We've used the English Standard Version in preparing this study, but other versions are fine to use. You might want to print the week's text from the internet, so that you can mark it up as you study it … refer to it often … meditate on it … memorize it … read it with all your heart and mind. We are taking in the living and active Word of God.

The **Commentary** comes next. This section helps explain the text and lays the groundwork for the questions and group discussion. The Commentary can be used in preparation and simply referred to if and when helpful in the group meeting. The same applies to each week's **History Heads Up**, which explores the historical context related to some aspect of the text. Nehemiah is a fascinating piece of geographical, archaeological, sociological, and political as well as theological history!

The previous steps lead to the **Questions to Consider**, which guide you through a careful examination and application of the biblical text. These questions enable you to dig in yourself and discover the riches of the Bible's words. The group discussion, then, will be even more profitable and encouraging.

GROUP MEETING

Each group meeting should open with prayer, reading of the Scripture text out loud (or selections from it, as you might want to skip some of those long lists of names!), and then the **Warm-Up**, which is simply a question or two to get the group thinking and talking about a central theme covered by the passage (about 10 minutes total).

Next comes the **Video** segment. The videos are personal introductions and guides to the passages—provided by Don Carson, Nancy Guthrie, and Kathleen Nielson (about 15 minutes total).

Leave ample time for the **Questions to Consider** (about 25 minutes total). As you discuss them together, these questions are designed to lead you into the biblical text—making observations, exploring the context, and drawing appropriate applications. Many of the questions involve looking at specific Bible verses, and it will often be helpful to have volunteers read aloud before you discuss. Don't worry if you don't get to all of the questions. Make as much progress as you can—and be ready to go back and study some more! Note: Depending on the dynamics of your group, from time to time you may want to switch the order of the Questions and the Video.

The **Wrap** is simply a time to "sum it up" and "pray it in"—whether using the prayer provided or simply praying in your own words, or both. In any case, do take time to pray about what you have studied as well as about the praises and requests you share with one another (about 10 minutes total).

As you leave, the **Looking Ahead** segment helps make the transition to the next chapters—hopefully inspiring thought and preparation in the intervening week.

ACKNOWLEDGMENTS

This study lays the groundwork for approaching Nehemiah. It is offered with prayers that those using it will press on to know and share God's Word with wisdom and fruitfulness. May we all grow in the Word, by the Spirit, to be mature disciples and make more disciples of our Lord Jesus Christ.

Thanks goes to P&R Publishing, who gave permission for me in this study to build on work begun in the Living Word study, *Nehemiah: Rebuilt and Rebuilding* (P&R, 2011).

I am thankful for all those around me who have encouraged me to keep on studying and sharing the Word—from the leaders of The Gospel Coalition, to local church pastors and leaders and friends, to my loving family—especially my husband, who shows me the love of Christ.

MEETING

NEHEMIAH

We are made to love stories—and Nehemiah draws us into a powerful one. It's a true story, all about God's faithfulness to His people and the call for their faithful response to Him. As Nehemiah leads the returned Jewish exiles to rebuild the wall of Jerusalem, it is clear God is watching over His people as He promised in His Word—and calling them to walk in light of that Word.

To get into this story, we need context. The Book of Nehemiah is not just about a leader who masterfully accomplishes the rebuilding of Jerusalem's broken-down wall. Nehemiah's people and city have a history. These are the people to whom God has made promises—promises that reach back to the beginning of the biblical story, as we'll see in this session.

The promises reach forward, all the way to us today. The Book of Nehemiah tells a crucial part of the story of redemptive history—our history, as Christians saved by the promised Christ who in the fullness of time was born of this people's seed. Nehemiah's restoration of a worshiping people tells our story, for the Old Testament system of worship points straight ahead to our Lord Jesus, through whom we have access to God. We must take this story personally. This lesson will help us get ready to take it in.

THE BOOK OF NEHEMIAH

Each session after this one will simply include a key verse from the week's passage, and you will then read the passage from your Bible. For this introductory session, find the Book of Nehemiah in your Bible and do a quick initial read-through of the entire book. Don't stop to analyze; we'll come back in more detail. For now, just aim to get a sense of the book as a whole.

COMMENTARY

Nehemiah gives us the Old Testament's final glimpse of God's gathered people. It's a personal glimpse, containing Nehemiah's own recorded words—compiled and expanded by an unidentified author, probably the author also of Ezra.

This final glimpse reveals a struggling remnant of Abraham's seed, his offspring. Through the generations after Abraham, that seed had grown into a great people just as God promised, in the land God promised (see Gen. 12:1-7). They had become a magnificent kingdom, and God had made a covenant with King David that in his line would come an eternal throne (see 2 Sam. 7:12-17). God's presence had dwelled with His people in the temple in Jerusalem, where according to the Law, priests regularly offered sacrifices to atone for the people's sin and people gathered joyfully on the prescribed feast days. But this chosen people had turned away from following the Lord and His law. In answer to their sin, God used the Assyrians and then the Babylonians to conquer first the Northern Kingdom of Israel and finally the Southern Kingdom of Judah. Jerusalem and its temple were destroyed, and the people were overthrown and dispersed as slaves into exile.

Ezra and Nehemiah both tell of the years following King Cyrus' decree in 538 B.C. releasing the exiles to return to their land. Three waves of Jewish exiles returned—the first led by Zerubbabel (recounted in Ezra 1–6), the second over 70 years later led by Ezra (see Ezra 7–10), and the third soon after, led by Nehemiah and described in his book. Ezra and Nehemiah, then, overlap: we will find Ezra in Nehemiah's story.

What about all of God's promises? That must have been the question asked by many of God's people at this low period in their history. Even when released from exile, they returned only as "slaves" (see Neh. 9:36) of the Persian Empire, to a broken-down city. Rebuilding was hard. Enemies surrounded them. Nehemiah is a great book for any of us who are struggling to walk ahead in faith according to God's Word.

The Book of Nehemiah shows that God's Word stands firm. God's steadfast covenant love to His people shows itself in amazing ways throughout Nehemiah's story. First of all, the fact that there still exists a faithful remnant of Abraham's seed is a great mercy and fulfillment of God's promises. Isaiah and Jeremiah both prophesied that a remnant of the Jews would survive the exile and return to the land. As we look up several Old Testament passages in this session, we'll see God's redemptive hand shaping all of this history.

God's covenant love to His people shows itself not just in their survival but also in His continuing provision of godly leaders who make clear the path of faith. No longer do these people have a king—although Zerubbabel as David's descendant represents God's sure promise of an eternal king in that line. There were post-exilic prophets sent by God: Haggai, Zechariah, and Malachi. There remained faithful priests, as in the case of Ezra, who "set his heart to study the Law of the LORD, and to do it and to teach his statutes and rules in Israel" (Ezra 7:10). Ezra led his group back to Jerusalem to rebuild the temple.

And then there were leaders like Nehemiah, called to specific tasks. God provides in Nehemiah a wise leader, from whom we can learn much about effective, godly leadership. Nehemiah's task is to bring God's people together at this point in history to rebuild—the wall, yes, but most importantly the people. Nehemiah aims to bring this people together within the city of Jerusalem so that they can live according to God's law—not just a compilation of rules but a system of worship that provides a means of coming as God's people into God's presence.

The Book of Nehemiah highlights God's merciful provision of that means, through the temple with its priests and sacrifices. There is great joy as the people reassemble within Jerusalem's walls, hear the Law, and reinstitute its prescribed worship. As they repent of their sin, and even as they fall into sin, we understand that we are reading about a God who in His unfailing love provides a way for His people to be forgiven. As we hear of sacrifices for sin offered by priests, we understand that this is the unfolding redemption story—one that culminates in Christ the Promised One who through His life and death and resurrection fulfilled the Law. These people were not able to fulfill it, nor are we; Jesus Christ was able. The Old Testament closes with assemblies of worship led by priests in Jerusalem; the New Testament opens four centuries later with the coming of the one great High Priest, who shed His own blood as the final, perfect sacrifice for sin. No longer do we need priests and sacrifices and temple; Christ has once and for all accomplished the purification of God's people toward which the sacrificial system pointed.

As we open Nehemiah, we can get ready to watch the God of history at work. We are reading the unfolding story of our redemption in Christ the Promised One who came, who died, who rose again, who ascended, who reigns, and who is coming again. In Christ the climax has come, but the story is not over. And we get to live in it, right now. Even in the midst of our struggles, we get to trust and obey the same faithful God and His same faithful Word. Nehemiah helps point the way.

HISTORY HEADS UP!

To watch these great ancient empires rise and fall helps put our own time in perspective. (It also helps us get Old Testament history straight!) The **Assyrian Empire** was the cruel regional super-power that conquered and dispersed the Northern Kingdom of Israel in 722 B.C. But the extensive Assyrian Empire eventually fell to the **Babylonians**, whose great King Nebuchadnezzar in 586 B.C. conquered the Southern Kingdom of Judah, ravaged Jerusalem, destroyed the temple, and took the people into exile (the "Babylonian captivity").

The Babylonians, however, in 539 B.C. fell to the Medes and the **Persians**, whose great empire began with the reign of King Cyrus. The Bible shows us God's sovereign hand shaping all this history according to His grand redemptive plan. Isaiah speaks of Cyrus as one whom God directs and equips, God's servant, even though he does not know God (see Isa. 45:1-6). How might this biblical perspective affect our view of nations in turmoil today?

WARM-UP

React together to your read-through of the Book of Nehemiah. What stood out to you?

What questions arose?

What do you hope to get out of your study of this book in the weeks ahead?

SHOW SESSION 1 VIDEO: MEETING NEHEMIAH

In this introductory video, Don Carson helps us sort out Nehemiah's place in history, especially in the history of redemption. Listen together to this informative introduction to the book and then share briefly one or two points you found interesting or perhaps brand new.

QUESTIONS TO CONSIDER

As you consider and then discuss these questions, aim to listen and encourage one another to listen with care and humility to the Word of God.

Think about Nehemiah as one whole book, one unified story. What main theme(s) do you find?

How does the plot seem to develop from beginning to end? For example, is there a climax, or high point, that stands out?

Evaluate the following suggested outline as a group. Would you change it? If so, how?

    Action Initiated by a Crisis (Chapters 1–2)

    Walls Rebuilt Physically (Chapters 3–6)

    People Rebuilt Spiritually (Chapters 7–10)

    Results of Revival (Chapters 11–12)

    Unraveling at the End (Chapter 13)

What are your initial observations of the man Nehemiah as you've encountered him in this quick read? What words and phrases would you use to describe Nehemiah?

_____

_____

_____

We can't jump into Nehemiah without reminding ourselves of who these people are whom Nehemiah leads in rebuilding the wall of Jerusalem. As you read the following verses, jot down notes and comments concerning the history and identity of these people:

Genesis 12:1-7 (to Abraham):

_____

_____

Exodus 19:3-6 (to Moses):

_____

_____

2 Samuel 7:12-16 (to David):

_____

_____

1 Kings 9:1-9 (to Solomon):

_____

_____

In one sentence, summarize who these people are.

_____

_____

_____

God called out this people, multiplied them, redeemed them from slavery in Egypt, gave them His law, and made them a great kingdom in the promised land. Yet in Nehemiah we find they've fallen far from such stature. Review the Northern Kingdom of Israel's fall in 2 Kings 17:5-15 and the Southern Kingdom of Judah's fall in 2 Chronicles 36:11-21. Using some words from these texts, how would you sum up what led to their kingdoms' fall?

_____

_____

_____

God's hand was on this people through whom He had promised to bless all the nations of the world. Look through Isaiah 44:24–45:7 and Jeremiah 25:11-12 in order to marvel at God's sovereign plan foretold through His prophets. In these passages, what specifics of this plan emerge?

_____

_____

_____

Now we're ready to see Ezra and Nehemiah in context. Read 2 Chronicles 36:20-23 and Ezra 1:1-5. From a human perspective, at this period of history a Persian king frees the Jewish exiles to return to Jerusalem. In fact, history shows us that Cyrus permitted many captured peoples to return to their respective homelands. But from the larger perspective of God's purposes, in what ways might you describe what is happening here?

As you've moved through this introduction to the Book of Nehemiah, what aspects of God stand out to you? List those attributes below, take time to meditate on them, and consider what difference it might make this week to focus your thoughts on the Lord God.

WRAP

- We've encountered Nehemiah as one whole book, one unified narrative.

- We've glimpsed Nehemiah's historical and scriptural context.

- We've begun to grasp the significance of Nehemiah as our story—about our faithful, redeeming God.

PRAYER

One of the best things to do with Scripture you've studied is to "pray it in." Take time to pray together about what you have studied, using either the following prayer or your own words.

Thank You, Lord, that You are the God whose promises never fail. Thank You for showing us in Your Word that You direct human history from beginning to end, for Your redemptive purposes. Every nation and every life is in Your sovereign hand. Thank You for preserving Abraham's seed according to Your promises. Thank You for providing a place and a way for Your Old Testament people to come to You, through the sacrifices of priests to make atonement for sin. We acknowledge before You that we are sinful and stiff-necked, just like Your people in the Old Testament. We repent of our sin and thank You for Your mercy in sending Your Son, who took on Himself the punishment for that sin so that we Your people can live finally forgiven, by faith in Him. We come to You now not through priests in a temple but through the blood of Christ who laid down His life for us. As we study Your Word, please help us to see You more clearly and to follow You with growing faith and prayerful obedience. In the name of Jesus we pray, and for His glory, Amen.

Share one specific way you can pray for one another this week. Finish by praying for one another, as you carry the blessing and challenge of God's Word into your lives this week.

LOOKING AHEAD

Session 2 will take us into the book, where we meet Nehemiah in action—not from a distance but up close, as he tells his story and lets us see his personal relationship with the God he serves. What do people reveal when they tell us their stories? Watch for what Nehemiah the narrator will reveal.

NOTES

ACTION

IN LIGHT OF GOD'S WORD

Nehemiah opens with a crisis that quickly precipitates the action of the book. As we hear Nehemiah tell his story quite personally in these first two chapters, we'll ask what his response to this crisis reveals about him—and about God. Nehemiah understands his crisis in relation to his God. His outward action grows out of inward communion with God and faith in God's Word.

In the first session we established that the Book of Nehemiah is about God's faithfulness to His people and the call for their faithful response to Him. This big theme of Nehemiah the book comes to life in Nehemiah the man. What a challenge to watch this person in action! As he lets us see him both inside and out, Nehemiah reveals a life lived in communion with God and in light of God's unfailing Word.

NEHEMIAH 1-2

> *"O LORD God of heaven, the great and awesome God who keeps covenant and steadfast love with those who love him and keep his commandments, let your ear be attentive and your eyes open, to hear the prayer of your servant that I now pray before you day and night for the people of Israel your servants … " (Nehemiah 1:5-6).*

COMMENTARY

We've studied the background, but Nehemiah doesn't give it to us; he just plunges into the story. These first two chapters have four sections, and the first is **the crisis**. Nehemiah, cupbearer (prominent and trusted assistant) to the Persian king in the capital city of Susa, asks for and receives news of the people and the city God had promised to bless. In short, Nehemiah's fellow Jews who have returned to Jerusalem are in trouble, and their city's wall is still broken down. From the start, Nehemiah's focus is not just the city but also the people. Here is a successful man well situated in the Persian court, where he could have just settled down and enjoyed himself. But he doesn't even introduce himself first; his thoughts are drawn to his people, God's people, there in Jerusalem. Nehemiah evidently knows there's a bigger story going on.

The second section brings **Nehemiah's prayerful response to the crisis** (see 1:4-11). Notice first of all just how full it is of Old Testament background. Nehemiah knows the history of Israel and the Word of God given to them through Moses—and he prays on the basis of that Word. He knows it, and he prays it, to the God who gave it. He repents and asks according to it. What a corrective for our too-often quick, shallow prayers! Apparently this period of seeking God in prayer lasted for four months, after which the scene in chapter 2 takes place.

The third section (see 2:1-8) brings **Nehemiah's wise plan of response to the crisis**—grown out of these months of prayer. In this dramatic scene in the presence of the king and queen, Nehemiah's sad face precipitates the conversation for which he has clearly prepared. Nehemiah is quick to clarify that King Artaxerxes grants all his requests because "the good hand of my God was upon me" (2:8). Think of God's hand in this story: to place Nehemiah in the Persian court to begin with; to grant him the king's favor and the king's ear; and to bless his request to return to Jerusalem, well-supplied, in order to help his people.

But think, too, of the wisdom of Nehemiah's response to God's providential hand. He was afraid (see 2:2), but he kept praying (see 2:4). And he carried out a well-conceived and bold plan—from his sad face to his careful wording to his specific requests for letters. He had a detailed proposal for the king, which he delivered with grace, humility, and clarity. We see here both the providential working of God's hand and the faithful response to God of His servant Nehemiah. For Nehemiah, faith in the Lord God calls forth a response of wise and purposeful service to Him.

The fourth section brings **Nehemiah's active response to the crisis** (see 2:9-20). The scene is no longer preparatory, in the court of Susa. This scene is suddenly on the ground (never mind the 1,000-mile journey), with Nehemiah arriving in Jerusalem and ready to go to work. His leadership is not abstract or distanced; he's up in the middle of the night inspecting the actual broken-down walls and clearly listening to the Lord's direction. He's right in the fray, addressing directly both the people who will do the work and the enemies who will try to stop them. And in all of it he's telling of God's hand and God's faithfulness. With God's hand on him, Nehemiah responds actively to the crisis in Jerusalem.

Nehemiah can inspire us to respond prayerfully, wisely, and actively as well, in every crisis and every day of our lives. First and foremost Nehemiah inspires us to look to the Lord God whose gracious hand is on us. Only by God's mercy can we respond to Him in these ways. Nehemiah's faith rests in the God who is working His merciful plan of redemption through these people—to bring through their offspring and to this very city the Savior who is Christ the Lord. Through the gates of this city would walk the Son of God, the One who would make His people acceptable to God through His sacrifice on the cross. Thank God for Nehemiah's faithful response to God. Thank God for God's faithfulness to His promises.

HISTORY HEADS UP!

Let's think geography for a moment. The Persian Empire at its height included a vast spread of land from the Mediterranean Sea all the way to present-day India, with its capital Susa just north of the Persian Gulf, in modern-day Iran. The "province Beyond the River" (see Neh. 2:7,9) refers to the "Trans-Euphrates," that is, land beyond the Euphrates River. This included the whole area of Syria-Palestine, several months' journey away from Susa and administered by a provincial governor or "satrap." Under him served local governors like Sanballat, governor of Samaria (to the north of Judah). Tobiah served as some sort of Persian official in Ammon (to the east of Judah). Clearly, these neighboring officials hated the thought of Judah rising to a position of strength, with its capital city Jerusalem rebuilt and fortified (see 2:10,19-20). How might it affect our perspectives on the news today, to glimpse the history of these regions still so full of turmoil?

WARM-UP
Nehemiah the man is a fascinating combination of utter humility and secure confidence. How do these qualities fit together in a godly person? What do you think are the keys to living with both humility and confidence?

SHOW SESSION 2 VIDEO: ACTION IN LIGHT OF GOD'S WORD

In this video, Nancy Guthrie covers the who, what, where, and when of Nehemiah 1–2, in which we see that the good hand of Nehemiah's great God was at work for His people who were in great trouble. After watching, briefly share your observations and responses.

QUESTIONS TO CONSIDER

As you consider and then discuss these questions, aim to listen and encourage one another to listen with care and humility to the Word of God.

The crisis that opens the book does not threaten Nehemiah's own personal well-being; it's far away from Susa. Recall the background on these Jewish people and God's promises to them (see Session 1, pages 17-18). Then consider:

Why was this crisis so heartbreaking?

What does it tell us about Nehemiah that this crisis broke his heart (1:1-4)?

Spend some time observing carefully the prayer in Nehemiah 1:4-11. How might you divide this passage into sections, and why do you think the sections are in this order?

What words or phrases stand out to you?

How does Nehemiah base his prayer on God's Word (see, for example, Deut. 4:25-31; 7:6-11)?

What challenges you about this prayer?

Nehemiah was emphatically a man of prayer. Sometimes, as in this passage, his prayers were offered swiftly—like a bullet (see 2:4). Many of us have likely sent up "bullet prayers" of our own—although we can't rely on them exclusively. How would you summarize what we can learn from Nehemiah's prayer life as we observe it in the first two chapters?

In what ways does the scene in Nehemiah 2:1-8 show us the involvement of both God's sovereign hand and human execution of a wise plan? (Contrast Nehemiah's approach with the one we see in Ezra 8:21-23. How do both men show faith, in their respective contexts?)

In Nehemiah 2:11-18, examine Nehemiah's initial approach to leadership in this task of rebuilding Jerusalem's wall. What do you notice about his actions and his words—and his heart?

God's people always meet opposition from the world around. Observe the nature and tactics of the opposition in Nehemiah 2:19-20. On what does Nehemiah base his response in this particular confrontation?

_____

_____

_____

Christians do not defend themselves today as a nation against other nations. From this nation of God's Old Testament people came the promised Christ, the Redeemer of His people from all the nations of the world. Take a look at Ephesians 6:10-20 and 2 Corinthians 10:4-6. Until Jesus comes again, in what ways do Christians battle now?

_____

_____

_____

How do we see Nehemiah wearing some of the same armor and wielding some of the same weapons that those New Testament writers describe (Eph. 6:10-20; 2 Cor. 10:4-6)?

_____

_____

_____

What armor and what weapons do you most need to learn to use, and why?

_____

_____

_____

WRAP

- We've met Nehemiah and seen his heart for Jerusalem and its people.

- We've observed a challenging combination of biblically-based prayer and wise, courageous action.

- We've seen how God's sovereign hand guides and protects His people.

PRAYER

Take time to pray together about what you have studied, using either the following prayer or your own words.

We thank You, Heavenly Father, for the privilege and joy of praying to You. We affirm with Nehemiah that You are the Lord God of heaven, the great and awesome God who keeps covenant and steadfast love with those who love You and keep Your commandments. Forgive us for our disobedience and our little love of You, we pray. Thank You that we can come to You boldly as Your people, through the blood of Jesus who died for us and who lives to intercede for us at Your right hand right now. Help us, we pray, to spend time communing with You, to let Your Word permeate our prayers, to come humbly and repentantly and regularly into Your presence. Pour out Your Spirit and Your wisdom so that we would live wisely and shrewdly in this world as Your people, accomplishing Your good purposes for us according to Your Word. We pray this not for our own glory and success but only for Yours. In the name of Christ our Lord, Amen.

Take a moment for each to share one personal request or praise and conclude by praying specifically for one other—using either long prayers or "bullet prayers."

LOOKING AHEAD

Session 3 will take us into the hard work of rebuilding. Nehemiah 3–4 offers a vivid picture of God's people at work. How should we view the work we offer up to the Lord, as His people? Be on the lookout for various attitudes and perspectives around and within you.

NOTES

LABORING FOR A

GOD WHO FIGHTS

FOR US

How do we as God's people work together for His kingdom purposes? How do faith and work go together? How do we face opposition to our work? Nehemiah 3–4 addresses all these questions and more. It's a vivid part of the narrative—even chapter 3, with its long list of various Jews doing various jobs. What a glimpse into the lives of real people doing real work, going after it with willing and unified hearts, and with competent organization.

Nehemiah 4 shows us God's people under attack, right in the midst of their building project. We can learn a lot from their response, under the leadership of one who encourages them to find help in just the right ways, first and foremost through trust in their faithful God. Nehemiah leads this work for God only because of his faith in the Word of God. God has made promises to this people, and Nehemiah leads the people to work boldly and faithfully in light of those promises.

NEHEMIAH 3-4

*" ... In the place where you hear the sound of the
trumpet, rally to us there. Our God will fight for us."
So we labored at the work ... (Nehemiah 4:20-21).*

COMMENTARY

This section of Nehemiah challenges us to think about what it means to work well in service to God. First, it means to work willingly. Progress is made quickly here, because, as Nehemiah reports, "the people had a mind to work" (4:6). They turned out to do it, and they did it. Work is actually a blessed activity, through which we reflect the image of God our Maker—the original worker in Scripture (see Gen. 2:2-3).

To work well in service to God also means to work as His people— as valued individuals and as a unified body of believers. Reading chapter 3, we can't help but notice the names of real, historical individuals recorded for us in Holy Scripture: each one was needed, and worthy to be written down for generations to read. But we must note as well the effect of all these names together, all these individuals joining in the task of rebuilding Jerusalem's wall: "So *we* built the wall," Nehemiah says (4:6; emphasis added). God calls out not just individuals but a people—first the descendants of Abraham but finally all those who by faith are redeemed through Abraham's promised seed, the Lord Jesus Christ. My identity in Christ is as a member of His body, the church, and any work I do for Christ, I do as a member of that body (see 1 Cor. 12:12-26). Once we have put our faith in Him, this is our eternal identity: we become part of God's called-out people.

The work of God's people demands humility, as many come together to serve the Lord to whom we all belong. In the lists of Nehemiah 3 appear those of the highest positions along with groups of more common laborers—all joining together to rebuild this city of God's promise. The proud Tekoite nobles in verse 5 are at this point an exception that proves the rule. Almost as if they are ashamed of their nobles, the ordinary men of Tekoa take on an additional section (see 3:5,27). In chapter 4 Nehemiah shows his leadership by leading the way in self-sacrificing and unceasing participation.

Without masterful organization, all the humble participation in the world could not make for the quick kind of progress we see here. Nehemiah knows that God's work must be done decently and in order. Be sure to note the structured progression of workers carefully described section by section in chapter 3—as well as the logic of the placement of many of them. Clearly, faith in God and ordered planning merge beautifully in this rebuilding project. Both the faith and the order are severely challenged in chapter 4.

To work as God's people means we will face scorn and opposition from the world. We see this dramatically in chapter 4, as leaders of the surrounding nations jeer and threaten these Jews who are rebuilding their broken-down walls. The wisdom and work of God often appear as foolishness to unbelievers (see 1 Cor. 1:17-25). But it is potent foolishness—foolishness that threatens—and so its opponents threaten back. Until Christ comes again, believers will be under attack. The apostle Paul makes clear against whom we Christians wrestle: not flesh and blood, but "spiritual forces of evil" (Eph. 6:10-12).

Nehemiah's response to opposition shows, finally, that he leads God's people in this work sustained by faith in the Lord God. Such faith does not mean less hard work, but it means that in all our work we know what Nehemiah knows: "Our God will fight for us" (4:20). This faith is demonstrated in the immediate and continued prayers of Nehemiah and his people in the face of opposition (4:4,9). This faith is demonstrated in Nehemiah's whole-hearted encouragement of his people: "Do not be afraid of them. Remember the Lord, who is great and awesome "(4:14). This faith is demonstrated even in Nehemiah's unrelenting planning in the face of conflict. Prayer and wit and sweat all merge in this scene. Verse 9 well summarizes the continuing combination of faith and hard work: "We prayed to our God and set a guard."

What a challenging picture for God's people today: excellent work in service to God as His people willingly and humbly come together, unified under a wise leader who orders them well and who teaches them to put their faith in the faithful Lord God, persevering even in the face of opposition.

HISTORY HEADS UP! ═══════════════

Nehemiah's plan apparently divided the several miles of wall into 41 sections, listed counterclockwise in chapter 3, beginning and ending with the Sheep Gate (see 3:1,32). The exact location of all the towers and gates is not known, but many have suggested diagrams and sketches of what the rebuilt wall looked like. Various excavations have uncovered portions of Nehemiah's wall, and it has long been accepted that the eastern side of the rebuilt wall was moved closer in and higher on the ridge overlooking the Kidron Valley than the original wall.[1] Nehemiah 3:8 says the workers "restored" Jerusalem; the chapter at times mentions rebuilding but repeatedly describes repairing—indicating that this quick work of 52 days (see 6:15) most likely involved a lot of patching and shoring up, probably using the rubble of the "broken down" wall to restore the structure—but certainly not to restore it to its original state. Imagine yourself there, amid all the sights and sounds, working away, say, between some goldsmiths on one side and a few perfumers on the other.

WARM-UP

Can you think of some examples of Christian leaders in your experience who weren't too proud to pitch right in with the work that needed to be done?

What are the effects of this kind of servanthood?

SHOW SESSION 3 VIDEO: LABORING FOR A GOD WHO FIGHTS FOR US

In this video, Kathleen Nielson takes us into the scene of God's people at work amid the rubble of Jerusalem's broken-down wall—and helps connect this scene to us today. Take a few notes, and briefly share your responses.

QUESTIONS TO CONSIDER

As you consider and then discuss these questions, aim to listen and encourage one another to listen with care and humility to the Word of God.

Observe carefully the categories, identities, and organization of the workers listed throughout Nehemiah 3. What details stand out to you?

How might this scene of work relate to the church today? Read 1 Corinthians 12:12-31 to find and identify common themes.

Examine the ways in which Nehemiah carries out his leadership of this people. What verses stand out in Nehemiah 3–4 in relation to Nehemiah as a leader?

We will miss the larger meaning if we simply try to learn lessons of service and leadership—helpful as those lessons are. The work here depends not on Nehemiah or his people but on the faithful God they serve. Make a list of the various truths these two chapters show us about the Lord God.

How does our view of God determine the ways we serve others? How does our view of God shape our response to opposition?

Rather than the swords, spears, and bows of Nehemiah 4, we believers now take up different battle gear as we serve as witnesses to the gospel of Jesus Christ throughout the nations. We noted that gospel armor in Ephesians 6:10-20. In Romans 13:11-14, what else stands out about the way Christians are now called to do battle?

Finally, to recall clearly just what all these battles (both in Nehemiah's time and ours) are about, read Philippians 2:1-10.

What did Jesus Christ, the ultimate Servant of God, do for us?

What is the end goal of all our service to Him?

How does this affect the way we serve day by day, as part of His body?

WRAP

- We've observed a vivid picture of God's people working together.

- We've acknowledged the opposition that faces God's people doing God's work.

- We've seen that the key is to trust the great and awesome God who fights for His people.

PRAYER

Take time to pray together about what you have studied, using either the following prayer or your own words.

Thank You, Lord, for this challenging scene of all God's people working wholeheartedly together to rebuild Jerusalem. Whether we're high or low in people's estimation, let each of us learn more and more to consider others better than ourselves, to give greater honor to the weaker members of Christ's body, and to give ourselves to the unity and the health of Your church. We know that these people in Nehemiah's day were rebuilding the city You promised to bless—and we know, even better than they did, just what that blessing would entail. Thank You, Lord, that from the seed of this people Jesus came, walking right into the gates of this city of Jerusalem. May all our labors grow from faith in You our faithful God, who according to Your Word sent Your Son, our Savior. May we serve as faithful witnesses to His glory, for the building up of Your church, until He comes again. In Christ's name we pray, Amen.

Take a brief moment to share any updates on things you've asked the group to pray about. Then offer one way you can each pray for one another throughout the week. Let the tone of your prayer be thanksgiving for what God has done for you in Christ and what He is still doing in and through you now.

LOOKING AHEAD

Session 4 will show us God's people facing further opposition, both from within and without. The temptation and threat are often nothing but fear. Be on the lookout this week for ways in which the Enemy might tempt you to be afraid—and ways in which the Word leads you to deal with fear.

---

1. Derek Kidner, *Ezra and Nehemiah: An Introduction and Commentary* (Downers Grove, IL: InterVarsity Press, 1979), 86-89.

NOTES

FEARING GOD

IN A FALLEN WORLD

Conflict in this fallen world doesn't just come once and then go away. We've been reminded of the armor of God that helps us persevere through many battles. Only God's faithful provision for us enables us to serve Him with faithfulness all the way to the good end.

These next chapters reveal threats arising not just from enemies outside but also from enemies within. Nehemiah 5 deals with unrighteous and disobedient behavior among the Jews, in relation to how they treat the poor among them. Nehemiah 6 brings a reprise of the enemies all around Jerusalem who are trying to block its restoration.

In dealing with these threats, Nehemiah's constant motivation is not to win against all odds. Neither is he motivated simply by the need for good moral behavior. This is a man filled with a much greater motivation: the fear of God and the glory of His name.

NEHEMIAH 5-6

So the wall was finished on the twenty-fifth day of the month Elul, in fifty-two days. And when all our enemies heard of it, all the nations around us were afraid and fell greatly in their own esteem, for they perceived that this work had been accomplished with the help of our God (Nehemiah 6:15-16).

COMMENTARY

We said at the start that the Book of Nehemiah tells us about God's faithfulness to His people, and the call for their faithful response to Him. Chapters 5–6 reiterate the need for God's people to respond faithfully to a faithful God who has given them His Word and made them His own.

It may seem like Nehemiah 5 offers an interlude in the rebuilding campaign, but in reality this conflict among God's people probably simmered over an extended period of time. Nehemiah may have confronted it later, after the wall was rebuilt, but he inserts the account here to show the kinds of opposition he and the people faced. The presenting issue is an economic struggle, a kind of struggle we know well today. The wives in particular (see 5:1) are probably pointing out that most of the men have been so busy rebuilding walls that they have no time for cultivating crops. There is simply not enough food and provision to go around. Rather than helping one another, however, the rich are exploiting the poor, cruelly mistreating them in their poverty and need. The Mosaic law speaks directly to such situations. We'll see how Nehemiah calls the people back to faithfulness to the Lord and His Word.

The narrative is dramatic, as we follow the events from the not-dispassionate perspective of Nehemiah himself, telling us the story. It is fascinating, for example, to imagine the process that unfolded within Nehemiah just in the course of 5:6-7. How shall we evaluate this kind of anger? What did

Nehemiah do in order to take counsel with himself (v. 7)? What can we learn from this godly leader? Although we must learn more than leadership lessons, these kinds of lessons do jump from the text and can be instructive in the context of the entire story. It is good to take to heart Paul's words about the Old Testament events serving "as examples to us" (1 Cor. 10:6), so that we might flee evil and follow only Christ. In this case, we can see that God used Nehemiah's righteous actions not only to call His people back to the path of obedience but also to ensure their survival, as the people from whom the promised Seed would come.

The theme of fear develops through these chapters in a powerful way, as the fear of God stands up against the fear of man. All of us know this struggle. We have to relish the clarity of Nehemiah's words to a disobedient people: "The thing that you are doing is not good. Ought you not to walk in the fear of our God to prevent the taunts of the nations our enemies?" (5:9). Nehemiah could have chosen any number of weighty arguments against the oppression of poor people. Why does he choose to put it this way? What is at stake? Their oppression of the poor is here equated with not walking in the fear of God, thereby inviting scorn not only for themselves but for God.

The centrality of fearing God emerges even more forcefully when in chapter 6 the surrounding enemies try hard to frighten Nehemiah, using a variety of low-down methods. The chapter ends with fear forced back on their own heads—because they glimpse the God who is to be feared (see 6:16). There are lessons here for all of us who so easily succumb to the wrong kind of fears.

The story is not just about human action; it is about human beings responding to God with the right kind of fear—fear that humbly acknowledges and obeys God because of who He is. Especially through his personal narrative, Nehemiah shows us a life lived in response to God. His interspersed prayers to God continue through these chapters, reminding us of his constant awareness of and communion with God. His anger is not just his own; it reflects his concern for the witness of God's name. The way he conducts himself as governor stems not from moralism but from the fear of God (see 5:15). Nehemiah is steeped in the Word of God and the presence of God. Here is a man who entrusts himself not perfectly but with great faithfulness to a God he knows is faithful to His people, as He has promised in His Word. Nehemiah fears this God and so fears nothing else.

HISTORY HEADS UP!

The Mosaic Law did not forbid loaning money and demanding some sort of pledge or interest for the loan. Nehemiah participates in the practice himself (see 5:10). However, in carefully examining Deuteronomy 24:10-15, for example, we see that the overriding concern is not the legality of loans but the care to be taken for one in need: never to take his cloak, and not to oppress a hired servant who is poor and needy. Deuteronomy 15:12 allows for a Hebrew man or woman to be sold into service to repay debts—although there is provision made for freeing all such persons every seventh year, and they are to be sent away furnished generously with provision. "As the Lord your God has blessed you, you shall give to him" (Deut. 15:14). Leviticus 25:35-43 also allows for such service but commands above all brotherly love and care for those of God's people in need. Here lies the people's offense, which Nehemiah had not initially recognized, and to which he responds with dramatic action.

WARM-UP

You've read the Scripture, and you know Nehemiah 5–6 is full of conflict. Before we dig in, stop and ask: what seems to be at the root of all this conflict?

SHOW SESSION 4 VIDEO: FEARING GOD IN A FALLEN WORLD

In this video, Nancy Guthrie walks us through the unrelenting opposition Nehemiah faced on many fronts and how God's faithfulness brought him through it all. As you watch the video, prepare to share a few brief responses.

QUESTIONS TO CONSIDER

As you consider and then discuss these questions, aim to listen and encourage one another to listen with care and humility to the Word of God.

Nehemiah 5 uncovers simmering social injustice, as the Jews' cruel treatment of the poor and needy among them is exposed. Read Nehemiah's response specifically in 5:8. Then read Deuteronomy 15:12-15. Both these passages say, in effect, "Don't forget …" What is the point being made in both of these passages, and why is it so important?

Chart the various steps of Nehemiah's response to this discovered injustice, in verses 6-13. For each step answer the question: Why is this step so critical?

Through chapter 5, Nehemiah is governed by the fear of God (5:9,15). How do his specific actions reveal such a fear?

How would you summarize the connection between our fear of God and our treatment of the needy around us? (Before answering this question, read again Leviticus 25:39-43.)

List the various attempts in Nehemiah 6:1-14 to derail the work of rebuilding and for each one note the nature of Nehemiah's inner and outer responses.

Derailing attempt	Nehemiah's inner response	Nehemiah's outer response

What can we learn here about responding to this kind of opposition?

In what ways does Nehemiah 6:15-19 offer a perfect conclusion to this section (and yet not utter resolution to the story)?

In the midst of the threats, what larger purposes of God show through?

Think a bit about fear and what makes you afraid. Recall Nehemiah 4:14. Read the following passages: Deuteronomy 6:13,24; Matthew 10:26-33; Hebrews 10:19-25. Meditate a bit on the wonder of fearing God and the confidence of approaching Him through His Son who came to banish all fear of His wrath by taking it on Himself, in our place. How does the fear of God change our fear of anything else?

Nehemiah 6 does not offer complete resolution to this section of the book. We have a sense that, even though Nehemiah has addressed the injustice practiced by his people in that place at that time, it's not over. Read Isaiah 9:6-7. Although God's people are called to address injustice every step of the way, what is the only and final solution to the conflict we see here, both within and without?

WRAP

- We've seen the threat of conflict from within God's people, as their ungodly treatment of the needy among them is exposed and addressed.

- We've encountered surrounding enemies' persistent efforts to bring down the people and the work of God.

- We've been challenged to face such conflicts by fearing the Lord God.

PRAYER

Take time to pray together about what you have studied, using either the following prayer or your own words.

God in heaven, we confess our tendency to fear many things, for the sake of our own safety and well-being, amid all the conflict of this fallen world. Forgive us for not remembering to look to You, the only One to fear. Forgive us for not seeing the needy around us in light of seeing You—and caring for them as You have cared for us. As we take in Your Word, cultivate in us an awe for You, our merciful Lord.

We humbly thank You that You made a way for us fallen human beings to fear You with confidence, not fearing the wrath You poured out on Your Son, in our place, on the cross. Grant us faith, we pray, to fear You rightly and to walk before You as Your redeemed people. Thank You for the example of saints before us, Your chosen people who received Your promises and acted on them with faith. Thank You for the story of Nehemiah, who feared You and faithfully served Your people through a dark time of waiting for the coming of Your Son. Thank You that He came. Even so, come, Lord Jesus. In His name and for His glory, Amen.

Share your personal prayers and praises, knowing that all of us are poor and needy ones—needing the prayers and encouragement of others.

LOOKING AHEAD

Session 5 will take us into the next section of the book, following the completion of the wall. Now we'll focus more explicitly on the people who did the rebuilding. We'll look at what is required to rebuild people, as opposed to walls.

NOTES

NOTES

COMING TOGETHER

AROUND GOD'S WORD

Once the walls are finished, the rebuilding task is not over. Biblical history focuses not so much on a secure place as on the people of God who dwell in that place. This is a helpful reminder for us, isn't it? In the midst of all our good programs and projects, we always need to remember the people—and people's urgent need to feed on and follow God's life-giving Word.

That's what these two chapters show us. After the final organizational details are attended to in chapter 7, the people come together for a great assembly in chapter 8. They gather not to celebrate the completion of the building project; that will come later, in chapter 12. First comes this assembly that gives God's Word to God's people. This is an "interior building project," one that involves lots of spiritual breaches being filled in order for the people to be solid, grounded in the Word of God. It's a kind of building project we desperately need to continue today.

NEHEMIAH 7-8

And all the people gathered as one man into the square before the Water Gate. And they told Ezra the scribe to bring the Book of the Law of Moses that the LORD had commanded Israel. So Ezra the priest brought the Law before the assembly, both men and women and all who could understand what they heard, on the first day of the seventh month. And he read from it facing the square before the Water Gate from early morning until midday, ... (Nehemiah 8:1-3).

COMMENTARY

At this turning point in the story, let's remember where we are. In the largest context, the Bible is telling the story of God redeeming a people for Himself according to His covenant promises that find final fulfillment in Jesus Christ. The Book of Nehemiah gives a vivid final Old Testament glimpse of the people through whom God chose to accomplish His plan. As we said, the fact that they still exist as a people after the long Babylonian exile is evidence of God's hand. Nehemiah in the first part of the book has done his best to protect this people within the rebuilt walls of Jerusalem, and now the focus moves to a different kind of rebuilding—a spiritual one.

Don't skip too fast over chapter 7. It looks like a bunch of lists—and it is, for the most part. The opening verses not only show Nehemiah's care in setting up productive order and godly leadership for the now-walled city, but they also show how poor and vulnerable is the city within its walls, with few inhabitants and no rebuilt houses. The city's rebuilt temple was so unimpressive compared to the former glory of Solomon's that some of the older people wept (see Ezra 3:12). What a far cry from the many prophetic visions of Jerusalem's coming glory! (See, for example, Isaiah 62.) That glory was still to come, and it was a glory much greater than the former glory—as prophets like Haggai pointed out during this post-exilic period (see Hag. 2:3-9).

But the remnant of returned exiles stands together as a testament to God's ongoing covenant promises. This explains why Nehemiah is so careful to number them again, enrolling them by genealogy, using and recording in chapter 7 an older list essentially the same as the one recorded in Ezra 2. Each name offers a testament to the faithful promises of God in blessing Abraham's seed. When chapter 8, then, brings together "all the people ... as one man," we understand better the significance of this assembled people coming before God—to hear His Word. Their lives depend on it. Nehemiah now disappears as narrator, not to return until later in the story. It's Ezra the priest who appropriately leads this worship service around God's Word.

The Book of the Law at the center of chapter 8 is the Torah, what we call the Pentateuch—the first five books of the Bible. These books instruct the people concerning their history and their Law, through words of revelation breathed out by God's own Spirit and written by Moses. This is the Word of the Lord. We, God's people now, can learn much from this scene of God's people centuries before Christ, for we need what they needed: to hear and respond to God's Word. First and foremost we see the centrality of the Word: both the leaders and the people themselves clearly know that it is God's Word they need. The people ask for it and revere it, and the priests and Levites devote themselves to reading and teaching it for hours and hours.

There are actually two days of Bible study and worship in chapter 8. As you observe them both, notice carefully all the details you can. Notice who attends these gatherings: on the first day "men and women and all who could understand," and on the second day the heads of families, who need even more study in order to lead their families according to God's Word— as they proceed to do in the ensuing Feast of Booths. Notice how long these gatherings last, and the order of events—especially the steps in the teaching process on the first day. First the book is read. Then (perhaps during various pauses in the reading) the Levites apparently move among the people helping them to understand (see 8:7-8). This help probably involved translation of the Hebrew, as most of the people at that time would have spoken

Aramaic. But it also involved explanations: "giving the sense" in verse 8 suggests the work of exposition, section by section of the text. What a beautiful picture of God's people gathered to study God's Word, under teachers who are prepared to help them understand.

If we try to observe outcomes of this study of God's Word, we will certainly mention "understanding" near if not at the top of our list. As we trace that word "understand" throughout the chapter, we can find great encouragement: God's people can understand God's Word. Not perfectly, of course. But better and better—with study and prayer and godly teachers and leaders, and of course with the enlightenment of the Holy Spirit who inspired the words in the first place.

Other outcomes are evident: sorrowful repentance, obedience, hunger to learn more … and, of course, joy! One of the most wonderful responses we can both observe and experience personally as we study this passage is that of joy—the joy of the Lord (see 8:10). This joy is rooted, in this passage, in knowing and trusting God through His Word. This joy gives strength. May we find more and more of this joy in the Lord as we His people come together around His Word.

HISTORY HEADS UP!

The background of the Jewish feasts is rich and beautiful. These assemblies took place in the seventh month, called Tishri, which according to the Law was a month of holy feast days for God's people. The first gathering occurs on the first day of the seventh month (see 8:2), which Leviticus 23:23-25 describes as "a day of solemn rest, a memorial proclaimed with blast of trumpets, a holy convocation"—known as the Feast of Trumpets. Many observe that there is no mention of the tenth day of this month, the Day of Atonement (see Lev. 23:26-32). But Nehemiah emphasizes a third feast, the Feast of Booths, which was to take place over a week's time, from the 15th to the 22nd of the seventh month (see Lev. 23:33-43). Here's what happens: the gathered people discover this feast through their reading of the Law, and then they proceed directly to obey the instructions they've read (see Neh. 8:13-18). The Feast of Booths celebrated God's protection of His people through the wilderness wanderings after their deliverance from Egypt; now, after the exile, God's people have again been delivered, and they again acknowledge His hand of deliverance and ongoing protection.

WARM-UP

Observe the scenes in Nehemiah 8. What catches your attention about how the people of Israel relate to God's Word?

SHOW SESSION 5 VIDEO: COMING TOGETHER AROUND GOD'S WORD

In this video, Nancy Guthrie explains the great value of the Word of God by walking through the way the people of God hungered for and engaged with it. As you listen, write down key points that challenge you.

QUESTIONS TO CONSIDER

As you consider and then discuss these questions, aim to listen and encourage one another to listen with care and humility to the Word of God.

What qualities of Nehemiah emerge in the first five verses of chapter 7?

Why is this combination of qualities such a potent one?

Chapter 7 is largely composed of a detailed list of names and numbers. Why was it important for Nehemiah to take the time and effort to reproduce the list of names here?

What details from verses 6-73 stand out to you, and why?

In the scene of the first assembly (8:1-12), highlight or write down the words or phrases related to understanding. Write down at least three observations concerning what we can learn here about understanding God's Word.

Consider the role of the leadership in this first assembly—Ezra first, along with many others mentioned. How have they prepared for this assembly?

In what ways do they wisely lead God's people during the assembly time?

As you read the whole of Nehemiah 8, make a list of what happens when God's people read and study God's Word. Include references to specific verses.

Take time to ponder your list. What does it make you think? What does it make you pray?

It is good to repent and to weep when we read God's Word. But at this point the leaders tell the people not to grieve but to rejoice—for "the joy of the LORD is your strength" (8:10). What can you learn about this wonderful verse from its context in the chapter and the book?

How might you testify to the truth of this verse in your own life?

WRAP

- We've celebrated God's faithfulness in preserving His people according to His promises.

- We've seen the central importance for God's people of reading and studying God's Word.

- We've observed the encouraging results of such reading and study, as God's people rejoice and obey.

PRAYER

Take time to pray together about what you have studied, using either the following prayer or your own words.

Sovereign Lord, we're amazed at Your hand on Your people, through all the centuries and even to this day. You know us, You call us, You deliver us, You count us—You love us, each one and all of us together as Your people. Thank You that from the beginning You spoke to Your people and gave them Your Word. Thank You that faithful men like Moses wrote it down through the inspiration of Your Holy Spirit. Thank You that through this Word You reveal Yourself and Your plan of redemption to us. Thank You that You make us able to hear and understand this Word, as with the help of Your Spirit we read and study and seek You with all our hearts. Thank You for good teachers and leaders to help us understand. May we increasingly love to hear Your voice in Your Word. May we listen well, understand more and more, obey more and more, and know more and more joy as a result. May we in these pages from beginning to end see more and more clearly the Lord Jesus—the Word who from the beginning was with God and was God, through whom all things were created. We worship You, Lord God. As Your people we praise You for Your merciful plan of redemption revealed in Your holy Word. We lift up Jesus and pray in His name. Amen.

Take time to share your requests and praises with one another, preparing to go your way rejoicing in God's Word and God's promises.

LOOKING AHEAD

Session 6 will take us into an amazing scene of repentance and confession. In preparation for next week consider: When, why, and how do you usually confess your sin before God?

NOTES

NOTES

RESPONDING TO GOD

ACCORDING TO HIS WORD

Do you recall the people being instructed not to mourn or weep, in response to God's Word—but to remember that the joy of the Lord is their strength (see Neh. 8:9-12)? The right time for mourning had not yet come. In Nehemiah 9–10, that time has arrived. It is the same month; this scene of confession takes place a few days after the people celebrated the Feast of Booths (see 8:13-18).

It is important to keep in mind the chapters that came before. What leads us into repentance? Too often, we are not moved to repent until either our wrong is uncovered or our situation has become hopeless. Here the repentance is a direct response to hearing and understanding the Word of God. It is repentance according to the Word of God. In fact, the prayer of confession here overflows with the Word!

We're watching a revival among God's people, as the Word by the Spirit declares truth, convicts hearts, and reforms both doctrine and practice. Our own prayers for revival can be well informed by the story of Nehemiah.

NEHEMIAH 9-10

> *"Now, therefore, our God, the great, the mighty, and the awesome God, who keeps covenant and steadfast love, let not all the hardship seem little to you that has come upon us, upon our kings, our princes, our priests, our prophets, our fathers, and all your people, since the time of the kings of Assyria until this day. Yet you have been righteous in all that has come upon us, for you have dealt faithfully and we have acted wickedly"* (Nehemiah 9:32-33).

COMMENTARY

It had been a month of feasting, worshiping, and celebrating in Jerusalem. It had also been a month filled with hearing the Book of the Law—and learning to understand and obey it. The people had just gone out to the hills and brought back tree branches with which they had constructed booths on their roofs and in their courts and in the square, all over the city, in order to celebrate the Feast of Booths as God had commanded it through Moses (see 8:13-18). And now, before they disperse, they gather for a final meeting, one of confession and repentance.

This confession is first of all prepared for and directed by their leaders. The leaders throughout this month prepared the people's hearts through the reading and teaching of God's Word. Doubtless other preparations grew from that process, including the people's clothing and appearance which outwardly portrayed their inward repentance (see v. 1). They had also "separated themselves from all foreigners" (v. 2; see History Heads Up). Clearly, this time of worship and confession was set apart as a crucial and climactic gathering. The Levites assembled to lead the people in three hours of reading from the Word and then three hours of worship and confession.

This confession is not just individual but also corporate confession. These people have been prepared to come before God as His people, to confess their sins. What a challenging scene, one that helps us realize just who we are as part of God's people and how much our own lives are bound up with those of our brothers and sisters in the body of Christ. My sin is my own before God, and yet my sin is part of the story of God's redeeming a people, through the blood of His Son. This scene should make us take the corporate confession we practice in our own worship gatherings seriously, as we confess our sins together, knowing that God through Christ redeems a people for Himself. We are a sinful people who need God's mercy, a people who repent because we want above all to glorify Him and together show forth His excellencies to a dark world from which we have been rescued.

This confession depends on God, not us. It is about God first—and then us. Often we tend to pour out before God words all about ourselves and how badly we've behaved and how sorrowful we feel and how great are our needs. This is not all bad. We can pour out our hearts before a merciful God. But that is not where this prayer starts. This prayer of confession does not depend on how awful the people feel. It focuses on God, first, and who God is. "Confession" can mean not only a laying out of sin but also a declaration of truth. The truth declared in this scene begins with God. The call to worship in Nehemiah 9:5 lifts up the people's eyes to an eternal, glorious, exalted God.

This confession re-tells what God has done. Of course, it gets across some of the things His people have done as well. But this prayer is shaped by a declaration of God's work across the sweep of redemptive history. The Bible offers many instances of passages where speakers or writers review Israel's history in order to make theological points—as in Psalm 78 and Stephen's speech in Acts 7. Nehemiah's people have just been reading some of their history in the Book of the Law. They would have started with Genesis, and so this prayer reflects their reading by beginning as well with worship of the God who made heaven and earth (9:6). This is the longest prayer in the Bible, and it follows Old Testament history from creation through the time of the kingdom and the prophets. Whereas we often tell our national histories out of pride and patriotism, this historical survey, like many others in Scripture, re-tells the history in order to lead to repentance. We cannot adequately see how far astray from God we are until we remind ourselves of who God is and of all He has done for His people.

This confession lays out the people's sin alongside the mercy of God. The recounting of God's faithful acts is interrupted by two large sections that confess the people's rebellion against Him (see vv. 16-21,26-31). Without excuse this prayer declares the disobedience of God's people throughout history to the present moment—and at the same time repeatedly tells of God's merciful deliverance.

This confession asks for mercy in light of God's mercy. As the prayer comes to its conclusion, these living proofs of God's deliverance confess their own sin and claim God's covenant love for them as His people. We as God's people can join in the celebration of God's merciful deliverance and claim that mercy in our own lives—now through the finished work of Jesus Christ His Son.

Finally, this confession leads to changed behavior. Chapter 10 lays out the promises made by the people to God, to walk in renewed holiness and obedience to the Law. As you analyze the nature of these promises, you will see that the great majority of them relate to maintaining the temple system, with its priests and Levites and offerings and sacrifices. This is not because Nehemiah was a stickler for ceremonial law. It is because he recognized that the center of Old Testament law is the temple system, the God-ordained means by which sinners were brought back into right standing with God.

We are watching a movement of revival and reformation. Now, if this changed behavior had "stuck," we wouldn't need the rest of the Bible's story! We'll see in the Book of Nehemiah just how long this renewed obedience lasts. We'll see just how desperately these sinful people need the temple system with its sacrifices for their sins. We'll be reminded that at the center of all our revivals and reformations must be repentance and faith in the way God has provided for us to come to Him. That way has now been made clear—through the cross. "And every priest stands daily at his service, offering repeatedly the same sacrifices, which can never take away sins. But when Christ had offered for all time a single sacrifice for sins, he sat down at the right hand of God, waiting from that time until his enemies should be made a footstool for his feet. For by a single offering he has perfected for all time those who are being sanctified" (Heb. 10:11-14).

HISTORY HEADS UP! ════════════════════════

We read in Nehemiah 9:2 that "the Israelites separated themselves from all foreigners." This was done out of a desire to obey the law they had been reading (see, for example, Deut. 7:1-5). Ezra had previously and passionately addressed this issue specifically in relation to intermarriage with unbelievers (see Ezra 9). It is important to understand this separation not as a matter of racism or cultural arrogance. It was a matter of preserving God's covenant people as a "holy seed" (Ezra 9:2) set apart for God, from whom God's Promised One would come. God explained this law right after giving it: "For you are a people holy to the LORD your God. The LORD your God has chosen you to be a people for his treasured possession, out of all the peoples who are on the face of the earth" (Deut. 7:6; see also Lev. 20:26). Foreigners who put their faith in Israel's God were welcomed, grafted into the Jewish people—as in the cases of Ruth and Rahab (see Ezra 6:21). Because God's Old Testament people were pre-served as a holy seed from whom Christ came, God's people now can be called, through Christ, "a chosen race, a royal priesthood, a holy nation, a people for his own possession, that you may proclaim the excellencies of him who called you out of darkness into his marvelous light" (1 Pet. 2:9).

WARM UP
Why is the call to worship in Nehemiah 9:5 a great starting point for confession of sin?

SHOW SESSION 6 VIDEO: RESPONDING TO GOD ACCORDING TO HIS WORD

In this video, Don Carson examines the confession of the people and the renewal of their covenant with God, drawing out critical lessons for how we relate to God. Briefly share your responses.

QUESTIONS TO CONSIDER

As you consider and then discuss these questions, aim to listen and encourage one another to listen with care and humility to the Word of God.

This prayer takes us right through biblical history. How would you make a brief outline for the history covered in Nehemiah 9:6-15?

What strikes you about the way this history is told?

In verses 6-15, how does every sentence begin? Make a list of the attributes of God that emerge from these verses.

_____

_____

_____

_____

The "But" in verse 16 stands out as significant. What words in Nehemiah 9:16-21 help define the sinfulness of the Israelites in the wilderness (and define sin in general)?

_____

_____

_____

_____

Find the other "But" that stands out in 9:16-21. What observations can you make here about the nature of God's response to His sinful people?

_____

_____

_____

Nehemiah 9:22-25 tells of God's people taking possession of the land He promised them—both east of the Jordan (Sihon and Og) and west. What words and phrases show not just the fulfillment but the *overwhelmingly abundant* fulfillment of God's promises to His people?

_____

_____

_____

The rest of chapter 9 traces Israel's history through the time of the judges and then rather quickly through the days of the kingdom to the days of Nehemiah. In the process of clearly confessing their sin, the people unfold the character of the Lord God to whom they now turn for help. In Nehemiah 9:26-37, find key words and phrases that tell us about this God who loves and redeems His people.

_____

_____

_____

Look back over the picture of the Lord God that emerges in the prayer of Nehemiah 9. Think about your response to this prayer. How does this picture affect your thoughts concerning confession and repentance?

_____

_____

_____

Read 1 John 1:5–2:2. How does this passage enlarge our understanding of confession?

The people move from confession to covenanting: they promise God to turn from their sin and "do all the commandments of the LORD our Lord and his rules and his statutes" (10:29). In what specific areas of their lives have they been convicted to change (see Nehemiah 10:30-39)? How are these areas still relevant to us today as believers in Jesus Christ?

WRAP

- We've grasped the importance of confession in the lives of God's people, as they are convicted by His Word.

- We've seen the foundation of confession to be God's merciful deliverance of a sinful people.

- We've observed the centrality of the Old Testament ceremonial worship system, ordained by God to provide a way into His presence through sacrifices that all point to the final, perfect sacrifice of His Son.

PRAYER

Take time to pray together about what you have studied, using either the following prayer or your own words.

Eternal God, we bless You according to Your Word: You are from everlasting to everlasting. Blessed be Your glorious name, which is exalted above all blessing and praise. You are the Lord, You alone. You have created all things, and You have provided Your people with overflowing riches—not just the abundant riches of our physical lives, but most of all the riches of Your promises to Your people. Thank You that You are a God ready to forgive, gracious and merciful, slow to anger, and abounding in steadfast love. Thank You that You have not forsaken Your people throughout history and to this moment. Thank You that You have instead poured out on us Your redeeming love in Jesus Christ Your Son, who took our sin and suffered and died in our place. We confess, O Lord, that we are truly a sinful people. We have stiffened our necks against You in a multitude of ways. We have not paid attention to You and to Your gracious Word to us. We have not always ordered our families and our worship of You in the light of Your Word. We have been selfish, greedy, and proud; we have often succumbed to gossip and malice; we have imagined that our nurtured bitterness is justified. We have defied You not only in things that we should not have done and should not have thought, but in things we have failed to do and think. Thank You that in Your mercy, when we confess You are faithful and just to forgive us our sins and to cleanse us from all unrighteousness. According to Your Word we thank You and ask You to help us walk in the light of that Word, through the power of our risen Lord Jesus and for His glory. Amen.

Now take some time to share your personal prayers and praises, knowing that our gracious and merciful God hears all the prayers of His people.

LOOKING AHEAD

Session 7 will show us continued good results of the people's turning back to God and to His Word. In preparation for next time, be thinking about scriptural signs of health that show God's people to be living and growing in ways that please Him.

NOTES

CELEBRATING!

A MOMENT OF JOY IN JERUSALEM

SESSION 7 ⎯⎯⎯⎯⎯⎯⎯⎯⎯⎯⎯⎯⎯⎯

Chapters 11–12 show ongoing results of a revived people. We've just come from scenes of turning back to God's Word, confessing, and reforming according to that Word. These next scenes confirm and continue the good work God is doing in this remnant of His people. Jerusalem's wall has been rebuilt. As a people set apart within that wall they are being rebuilt spiritually, through leaders who teach God's Word and encourage faithful participation in worship according to the Law.

We are right to look for results of such rebuilding—discernible fruit that grows from times of revival. In Nehemiah, three results are clear and clearly presented one after the other: a repopulation program; a worship celebration; and an institutionalization. For the remnant of God's people in Jerusalem, these three results indicate spiritual health and growth. As we study these chapters, it will be worth asking how these results might correspond to signs of health and growth in God's people today.

NEHEMIAH 11-12

*And they offered great sacrifices that day and rejoiced,
for God had made them rejoice with great joy; the
women and children also rejoiced. And the joy of
Jerusalem was heard far away (Nehemiah 12:43).*

COMMENTARY

Nehemiah 11 describes a carefully organized repopulation program for the city of Jerusalem. There's a problem: this "holy city" (vv. 1,8) is a deserted, broken down ruin. They've got the wall rebuilt, but now they need some people to live inside and restore the city to life. The opening verses of chapter 11 make clear that nobody wanted to live in Jerusalem, as opposed to dwelling in the towns and farms around—and so they cast lots and showered blessings on any who were chosen and/or willing to set up homes in Jerusalem's rubble.

The situation would be hard enough for poor citizens returning to any broken-down city. But this is not any old broken-down city; this is Jerusalem. Why is Jerusalem called the "holy city"? Well, if we were like Nehemiah's people and had just been reviewing their history, we would better recall the significance of this city containing the temple where the Lord God had actually promised to dwell with His people. It was King David who with great rejoicing brought the ark of the covenant to Jerusalem and wanted to build God a house, but God said it would be David's son Solomon who would build the temple—and that God would make David a house that would last forever (see 2 Sam. 7:1-16). At the dedication of King Solomon's temple, the glory of the Lord filled that temple with such an overwhelming cloud of God's presence that "the priests could not stand to minister" (1 Kings 8:10-11). The temple on Mount Zion in Jerusalem was the place of God's presence to which all His people had streamed regularly, from all over the land, to offer sacrifices and celebrate the feast days according to the Law.

In rebuilding the wall and the people, Nehemiah aims ultimately to bring the people back inside and to bring life and worship back to this holy city. Back in Nehemiah 7:4, right after the wall was finished and as he was appointing guards and gatekeepers, Nehemiah showed his concern: "The city was wide and large, but the people within it were few, and no houses had been rebuilt." So chapter 11 brings the repopulation program, for the job is not done; Nehemiah will restore Jerusalem. In doing so, Nehemiah aims to restore the city of David and the center of God-ordained sacrifice, thus truly ending the exile by bring God's people back to the place of communion with Him.

Of course, the glimpse of restoration that comes in these chapters is fleeting. We still have to come to the end of the Book of Nehemiah. And even the desolate setting of this deserted city reminds us that the promised restoration is not to come through the quickly-rebuilt temple and wall. Yes, Jerusalem is promised to God's people as a place of eternally glorious worship in God's presence. Just take a peek into Isaiah 65:17-25. But New Testament believers know that Jesus Christ came and spoke of *Himself* as the temple, the temple that would be destroyed and then raised up again in three days (see John 2:18-22). Christians get to see the fulfillment of God's promise to dwell with His people, in Christ our God made flesh, and now through His Spirit—and finally forever in the "new Jerusalem" that the apostle John saw coming down out of heaven from God (see Rev. 21:1-3).

Only through Jesus, "God with us," does full and final restoration come. But we do get to glimpse it here, as God's people for a brief shining moment light up Jerusalem with their grand worship celebration. After the repopulation program in Nehemiah 11, we come to the dedication of the wall in chapter 12. Finally, after their work of rebuilding and after their study of God's Word and their repentance and reformation in light of it, they are ready. They are ready to dedicate the wall with renewed hearts of worship and with renewed commitment to the means of worship God provided for them. The documentation of priests and Levites that begins chapter 12 shows the importance of the temple system of worship, as prescribed by the Law. As we look into this worship celebration, however, we find not just conformity to the Law. We find the joy of the Lord. We also see the witness possible through joyful worship.

Nehemiah 12 concludes with institutionalization, that is, with setting up structures necessary for the continuity of such worship as we have seen. We've noted in earlier chapters the intentional and even orchestrated leadership at the helm of these gatherings. The leaders are not simply waiting for something to happen, moment by moment. Granted, after such profound and glorious worship gatherings, the final section of chapter 12 might seem a little pedantic, perhaps a bit of a letdown. But we notice here not only carefully structured provision for worship, according to the Law. We also notice—right in the midst of all the appointments of certain portions for certain people in certain places—joy (see 12:44). The benefit of all the great gatherings that have taken place must not be left behind; that benefit must instead be consolidated and carried on, in the more measured but still joyful rhythm of ongoing daily life and worship. Just so, the apostle Paul could both speak eloquently about being strengthened by the grace that is in Christ Jesus, and remember finally to tell Timothy to bring him his cloak and books and parchments (see 2 Tim. 2:1; 4:13).

As we observe Nehemiah restoring Jerusalem and its temple worship, we must continually remind ourselves of what the Old Testament ceremonial system pointed toward: Jesus Christ our great High Priest, our Temple, the One who brought God's presence to us, and who through His death and resurrection brings us near to God. In the promised New Jerusalem, there is no temple, "For its temple is the Lord God the Almighty and the Lamb" (Rev. 21:22). In the Old Jerusalem, however, until the coming of Jesus the temple was God's good provision, a means for His people to worship Him, and a picture of the Savior to come.

HISTORY HEADS UP! ════════════════

We continue to learn a lot of names of people from various families and tribes of Israel in these chapters. This remnant may have included representatives from most or even the entire original twelve tribes descended from the sons of Jacob. But the great majority comes from three tribes—Judah, Benjamin, and Levi—all of whom from the time of Joshua had settled in the area that eventually became the Southern Kingdom of Judah, where Jerusalem was located. We know that the tribe of Judah was the kingly tribe of David, from which Jesus came. What about the Levites, so central to the story of Nehemiah and its worshiping people? As explained in Deuteronomy 18:1-8, the tribe of Levi was chosen to minister to God's people (the sons of Aaron as priests and the rest of the Levites in various ministry roles). They received no tribal inheritance of land, for "the LORD is their inheritance." The law provided, however, that those ministering should be supplied by tithes and offerings regularly offered by the people, as we see happening in Nehemiah 12:44-47.

WARM-UP

Christians do not need Jerusalem, or a temple, or priests to worship now; we have continual access into God's presence through Christ our Savior. But we do have ordained leaders and regular worship gatherings of the church. How might the worship we see in these chapters stimulate our thinking about the worship of our congregations today?

SHOW SESSION 7 VIDEO: CELEBRATING! A MOMENT OF JOY IN JERUSALEM

In this video, Kathleen Nielson unfolds the results of revival evident in God's people—centering in the worship celebration dedicating the rebuilt wall. Briefly share your comments and observations.

QUESTIONS TO CONSIDER

As you consider and then discuss these questions, aim to listen and encourage one another to listen with care and humility to the Word of God.

The commentary briefly reviews the significance of Jerusalem for the people of God and the importance of repopulating it—as they begin to do in Nehemiah 11:1-2. Look through chapter 11 in your Bible, noting the tribes and categories of people represented. Then read Psalm 48. What strikes you in this beautiful poetic celebration of "the city of our God"?

The first portion of chapter 12 spends so much time listing the priests and Levites because they were essential to the worship we are reading about. God preserved this tribe through the exile and is now reestablishing them as the spiritual leaders of His worshiping people. In Nehemiah 12:27-30, what insights can we glean about the roles of the Levites and the nature of the worship?

In Nehemiah 12:31, Nehemiah the narrator is back! From verses 31-40, summarize the plan or make a quick sketch of the dedication ceremony Nehemiah organizes.

As they walked on those walls, what sorts of thoughts might have been going through the minds of these people who had rebuilt them?

Trace the role of music in the worship celebration in verses 27-43. What and how does music contribute to worship, here in the text and in your own experience? (See also Psalm 150.)

Now trace joy, gladness, and thanksgiving through verses 27-44, observing everything you possibly can about joy from the text. Recall what we learned of joy in chapter 8. What lessons should we take away from Nehemiah regarding joy?

How will you, or could you, respond to what you've learned in Nehemiah about joy? To what areas of your life might this apply first?

What kinds of organization take place in 12:44-47, and why are they so important?"

Consider the various ways Nehemiah 12 shows the outcomes of hearing and learning the Book of the Law. Why must God's worshiping people be God's Word-filled people?

What happens if we're not?

What happens if we are?

WRAP

- We've seen God's people obediently restoring the city of Jerusalem as the center of God-ordained worship.

- We've witnessed the joy given by God to His worshiping people—joy that echoes far.

- We've noted the people's faithful support and maintenance of the structures necessary for worship according to God's Law.

PRAYER

Take time to pray together about what you have studied, using either the following prayer or your own words.

Heavenly Father, we worship You. Thank You that You have taught Your people in Your Word just how to worship. Thank You for this reminder of how from the beginning You made a way for Your people to come into Your presence. Thank You that You provided the temple and priests and sacrifices in Jerusalem—but thank You most of all that Jesus Christ came to fulfill all that those Old Testament institutions pointed toward. Thank You that Jesus is our temple; we come to You in Him. Thank You that Jesus is our High Priest who offered Himself as the full and final sacrifice for our sin; we claim His death on our behalf. In Christ our Lord we worship You. Forgive us for our half-hearted and imperfect worship. Help us, we pray, to know both great times of revival and steady times of daily and weekly worship, as we follow and fill ourselves with Your Word. Help us to learn more and more, as Your people, to worship You joyfully in spirit and in truth. For the glory of Christ we pray, Amen.

Conclude by sharing your requests and praises, praying for one another as you go out to live God's Word.

LOOKING AHEAD

Many have pointed out how nice it would be if the Book of Nehemiah ended with chapter 12. Have you read about or even experienced times of revival that were followed by times of falling away? Why does this happen?

NOTES

LEANING FORWARD IN THE DARK

A FAILED REFORMATION

Just as the book opened with Nehemiah's first-person narrative, so it ends—with his powerfully personal response to the weakening of the reformation that occurred among these returned exiles. It is a disappointing end to an inspiring story. It is a dark end to Old Testament history. It is an end that makes us long for the rest of the biblical story.

Although the timeline of all these events is not completely clear, we know that after 12 years as governor of Judah, Nehemiah left Jerusalem to return to Susa for an extended period of time. He then returned to Jerusalem to discover the evil he confronts in this last chapter. These confrontations help us come face to face with the sinful desires and practices of all of us, even now. They also move us to claim God's gracious forgiveness in Christ and God's power in us, through the risen Christ, to turn from evil and serve Him faithfully, again and again, until Jesus returns.

NEHEMIAH 13

Remember me, O my God, concerning this, and do not
wipe out my good deeds that I have done for the house
of my God and for his service.
… Remember this also in my favor, O my God,
and spare me according to the greatness of your
steadfast love.
… Remember me, O my God, for good
(Nehemiah 13:14,22,31).

COMMENTARY

The book leaves us with failure. We've seen God's people revived by God's Word as they've read and studied it, confessed according to it, and aimed to obey it in lives of ongoing worship. They understand who they are in light of that Word: a people chosen by God, blessed by His promises, called to be holy and set apart unto the Lord (see Deut. 7:6-11). Here at the end of the book, many of them fail spectacularly in that calling. Nehemiah 13 shows us their failure of holiness in three major categories.

First, the people fail to be holy in relation to the temple in Jerusalem, the very center of their lives as God's worshiping people. Chapter 13 begins with an initial section that seems to show the people's obedience to the Law, evidently referring to Deuteronomy 23:3-5 which commanded that Ammonites and Moabites be excluded from the assembly of God. The people appear to obey—with action reminiscent of Nehemiah 9:2, and, farther back, Ezra 9–10. However, they are not paying careful attention to God's Word. We might see a new legalism suggested here, as they separate from Israel "all those of foreign descent" rather than just the two nations named (see 13:1-3). We know that they do not separate completely from these two nations, because we know that Tobiah is an Ammonite—this Tobiah who according to verses 4-5 has taken up residence right in the temple! We've met this enemy of the people of God earlier (see 2:10; 4:7-8).

As we study Nehemiah 13:4-14, we'll see that the Jerusalem temple has been polluted and forsaken in many ways. The tithes and portions are no longer being given by the people to the Levites, who have now fled from temple work to make a living in the fields. The storeroom that should hold these tithes and offerings holds … Tobiah. And so cleansing is needed. We'll watch Nehemiah's response. And we'll wonder, too, how this neglect of the house of God might relate to us. How might we be drawn to forsake or neglect God's people and the lives of wholehearted worship we are called to live together?

Second, the people fail to be holy in relation to the Sabbath (see 13:15-22). Foreigners are bringing their goods into Jerusalem on the Sabbath, and the Jews are buying. Profit has triumphed over purity. This part of the Law was a major concern to Ezra and Nehemiah and many of the prophets throughout Israel's history—which Nehemiah alludes to in verse 18: "Did not your fathers act in this way, and did not our God bring all this disaster on us and on this city? Now you are bringing more wrath on Israel by profaning the Sabbath." Does this seem petty—worrying about shopping on the Sabbath? Does it seem like Nehemiah is making a big deal about letting one guy have a room in the temple? Why are these laws so hugely important? Nehemiah's response shows that they are.

Third, the people fail to be holy in relation to marriage (see 13:23-29). We have seen that God's people were to welcome foreigners who put their faith in Israel's God, but we have seen as well that God's people were not to intermarry with foreigners who worshiped false gods—as did all the nations around them. This failure brings perhaps the most vehement response of Nehemiah. Why is this?

God set apart this people for His redemptive purposes. As we reach the close of Old Testament history, we cannot forget the scope of that history— of which the people's prayers of confession have reminded us. These are the descendants of Abraham, the one to whom and through whom God promised blessing. These are the descendants of Moses, through whom God gave the Law these people have been reading. These are the descendants of King David, who helped shape the worship we see here—and who in this very city received God's promise that His throne would be established forever. All this history and all these promises are revealed in the Scriptures: God gave His Word to light the way. Nehemiah understands that God's Word is to be passed on generation by generation, through faithful leaders and teachers and worshipers and families who keep studying and teaching it—and living according to it. Nehemiah will not stand by and see the end of that passing on. Yet he knows, in the end, that the only one to trust is God Himself, the God of steadfast love whose Word does not fail. Nehemiah ends in the dark with only God to trust. And God is faithful.

The biblical story does not end in darkness. Through the death and resurrection of the promised, holy Son of God who came, the people of God from all the nations are made holy, as they put their faith in Him. In light of the Bible's complete revelation, we understand that Jesus is the light Nehemiah yearned for. He is the One to whom all the Law and Prophets point. The light has shined. Yet even as we, God's people of the new covenant, walk according to that light, we still walk through darkness. Our reformations still fail. We're still waiting for the full light of day when Jesus comes again. And we can still trust Him, believing in His Word. And we can keep passing it on, until that day.

HISTORY HEADS UP! ═══════════════════════════

It is interesting to consider the legacy left by these early generations of returned exiles, with leaders like Zerubbabel, Ezra, and Nehemiah, along with the post-exilic prophets Haggai, Zechariah, and Malachi. The period we call Second Temple Judaism began with Zerubbabel's rebuilt temple during the early days of the Persian Empire, and extended through the Persians, the Greeks, the Maccabeans, and finally the Romans—until 70 A.D., when the Romans destroyed Jerusalem and its temple. There is no doubt that, during the early centuries of the Second Temple Era, many Jews became a people of the book. They intently studied, copied, compiled, and taught the Scriptures. As the New Testament opens, we find in the scribes and the Pharisees of the Gospels this enduring emphasis on study and knowledge of the Word— although elitism and legalism had corrupted many of the leaders. Jesus came and showed us how the whole Word, from beginning to end, points to Him.

WARM-UP

We've come to the end of the Book of Nehemiah. It's a good time to look back and ask, "What is it that has struck me about this book as a whole?" How would you answer that question?

SHOW SESSION 8 VIDEO: LEANING FORWARD IN THE DARK: A FAILED REFORMATION

In this video, Don Carson talks about the brutal realism with which the Book of Nehemiah ends—rules more prominent than obedience, family ties more important than covenantal faithfulness, attitudes more secular than spiritual, profit of greater importance than purity. Share your responses.

QUESTIONS TO CONSIDER

As you consider and then discuss these questions, aim to listen and encourage one another to listen with care and humility to the Word of God.

First, compare and contrast the people's promises in chapter 10 with the reality in chapter 13. Compare Nehemiah 10:32-39 with 13:4-14.

Compare Nehemiah 10:31 with 13:15-22.

Compare Nehemiah 10:28-30 with 13:23-29.

What patterns emerge?

What impulses or desires in the leaders and the people might have contributed to the failures seen in these verses?

How do Christians struggle today against such impulses as well?

_____

_____

_____

Although we worship together as God's people, we New Testament believers do not have a temple like the one Nehemiah was eager to restore in Jerusalem. We do not regard the Sabbath regulations in exactly the same way, although we celebrate the Lord's Day. We do not forbid marriage with people from other countries, although we hold certain beliefs about Christian marriage. How do the following New Testament verses unfold some of the same principles we've seen at work in Nehemiah? *(Look into these verses not to explain them completely but to get the thrust of them.)*

2 Corinthians 6:14-18 (in regard to marriage)

_____

_____

Matthew 5:17; Matthew 12:1-8 (in regard to the Sabbath)

_____

_____

2 Corinthians 9:6-15; Hebrews 10:19-25 (in regard to worship and tithing)

Find the repeated noun in verses 7, 17, and 27, and the repeated verb in verses 11, 17, and 25.

Repeated noun:

Repeated verb:

How would you summarize Nehemiah's approach in this chapter?

How do you respond to his methods?

Observe Nehemiah's repeated prayer to God in this final chapter, with all its various wordings. How does this prayer point both to the darkness and the light here at the end of Nehemiah's story and of Old Testament history?

_____

_____

_____

_____

Think back on the Book of Nehemiah as a whole. Looking back at the very first chapter, what themes do you find planted there that the book develops throughout?

_____

_____

_____

_____

Nehemiah has shown us the big theme of God's faithfulness to His people according to His Word, and His call for our faithful obedience to Him. What parts of that theme have touched you most personally, and why?

_____

_____

_____

_____

Which verses or passages have especially stood out to you, and why?

What does this book inspire you to pray—for yourself and for the body of Christ around you?

WRAP

- We've seen the failure of God's people to obey God's law—that is, we've seen their need for a Savior.

- We've seen our own sinful desires and struggles reflected in these people.

- We've followed Nehemiah's gaze toward the God of steadfast love— the God who fulfilled all His promises by sending His own Son to save us.

PRAYER

Take time to pray together about what you have studied, using either the following prayer or your own words.

Lord God, as we conclude this study we see clearly both the certainty of Your promises and also the sinfulness of Your people to whom You have given these promises. Thank You for Your Word which shows us Yourself and shows us ourselves. Thank You that all the promises Nehemiah was holding onto in the dark burst into fulfillment with the coming of the promised Christ, our Lord and Savior. We praise You for Your faithfulness. We ask humbly that You help us, Your redeemed people, to walk according to Your Word until Jesus comes again. Help us to teach it well to the next generation. When we fail, Lord, which we will do, please help us to confess our sins to You and to know Your forgiveness through Jesus who died for us. Please help us, by the Spirit of the risen Christ in us, to walk more and more faithfully, being conformed to His image day by day. Thank You for Your promise to help us in these ways. May we as Your joyfully worshiping people show the light of Jesus to a dark world. To You be glory in the church and in Christ Jesus throughout all generations, forever and ever. Amen.

Conclude with prayer for one another one more time, thanking God and committing one another to His care.

NOTES

NOTES

Welcome to Community!

Meeting together to study God's Word is an exciting adventure. A small group is a group of people unwilling to settle for anything less than redemptive community.

CORE VALUES

COMMUNITY: God is relational, so He created us to live in relationship with Him and each other. Authentic community involves sharing life together and connecting on many levels with others in our group.

GROUP PROCESS: Developing authentic community takes time. It's a journey of sharing our stories with each other and learning together.

INTERACTIVE BIBLE STUDY: We need to deepen our understanding of God's Word. People learn and remember more as they wrestle with truth and learn from others. Bible discovery and group interaction enhance growth.

EXPERIENTIAL GROWTH: Beyond solely reading, studying, and dissecting the Bible, being a disciple of Christ involves reunifying knowledge with experience. We do this by taking questions to God, opening a dialogue with our hearts, and utilizing other ways to listen to God speak. Experiential growth is always grounded in the Bible as God's primary revelation and our ultimate truth-source.

POWER OF GOD: Processes and strategies will be ineffective unless we invite and embrace the presence and power of God. Jesus needs to be the centerpiece of our group experiences and the Holy Spirit must be at work.

REDEMPTIVE COMMUNITY: Healing best occurs within the context of community and relationships. It's vital to see ourselves through the eyes of others, share our stories, and ultimately find freedom from the secrets and lies that enslave our souls.

MISSION: God has invited us into a great mission of setting captives free and healing the broken-hearted (Isaiah 61:1-2). However, we can only join in this mission to the degree that we've let Jesus bind up our wounds and set us free.

Leading a Small Group

You will find a great deal of helpful information in this section that will be crucial for success as you lead your group.

Reading through this section and utilizing the suggested principles and practices will greatly enhance the group experience. First is to accept the limitations of leadership. You cannot transform a life. You must lead your group to the Bible, the Holy Spirit, and the power of Christian community. By doing so your group will have all the tools necessary to draw closer to God and to each other, and to experience heart transformation.

MAKE THE FOLLOWING THINGS AVAILABLE AT EACH SESSION:

+ *Rebuild: A Study in Nehemiah* Bible study for each attendee
+ Extra Bibles
+ Snacks and refreshments (encourage everyone to bring something)
+ Pens or pencils for each attendee

THE SETTING AND GENERAL TIPS

#1 Prepare for each meeting by reviewing the material, praying for each group member, asking the Holy Spirit to join you, and making Jesus the centerpiece of every experience.

#2 Create the right environment by making sure chairs are arranged so each person can see every other attendee. Set the room temperature at 69 degrees. If meeting in a home, make sure pets are where they cannot interrupt the meeting. Request that cell phones be turned off unless someone is expecting an emergency call. Have music playing as people arrive (volume low enough for people to converse).

#3   Try to have soft drinks and coffee available for early arrivals.

#4   Have someone with the spiritual gift of hospitality ready to make new attendees feel welcome.

#5   Be sure there is adequate lighting so that everyone can read without straining.

#6   Think of ways to connect with group members away from group time. The amount of participation you have during your group meetings is directly related to the amount of time you connect with your group members away from the group meeting. Consider sending emails, texts, or social networking messages during the week encouraging them to come next week and to expect God to do great things throughout the course of this study.

#7   Don't lose patience about the depth of relationship group members are experiencing. Building authentic Christian community takes time.

#8   Never ask someone to pray aloud without first asking their permission.

LEADING MEETINGS

#1   Before the Warm Up sections, do not say, "Now we're going to do a warm-up activity." The entire session should feel like a conversation from beginning to end, not a classroom experience.

#2   Be certain every member responds to the group questions. The goal is for every person to hear his or her own voice early in the meeting. People will then feel comfortable to converse later on. If some members don't have an answer, encourage them to listen as others respond and then revisit the question on their own later.

#3   Remember, a great group leader talks less than 10 percent of the time. If you ask a question and no one answers, just wait. If you create an environment where you fill the gaps of silence, the group will quickly learn they don't need to join you in the conversation.

#4   Don't be hesitant to call people by name as you ask them to respond to questions or to give their opinions. Be sensitive, but engage everyone in the conversation.

#5   Don't ask people to read aloud unless you have gotten their permission prior to the meeting. Feel free to ask for volunteers to read.

#6   Watch your time. If discussion extends past the time limits suggested, offer the option of pressing on into other discussions or continuing the current content into your next meeting. REMEMBER: People and their needs are always more important than completing your agenda or finishing all the questions.

NOTES